WETLANDS

Rose Pipes

A ZOË BOOK

A ZOË BOOK

© 1997 Zoë Books Limited

Devised and produced by
Zoë Books Limited
15 Worthy Lane
Winchester
Hampshire SO23 7AB
England

First published in Great Britain in 1997 by
Zoë Books Limited
15 Worthy Lane
Winchester
Hampshire SO23 7AB

A record of the CIP data is available from the British Library.

ISBN 1 86173 017 9

Printed in Italy by Grafedit SpA
Editor: Kath Davies
Artwork: David Hogg
Map: Sterling Associates
Design & Production: Sterling Associates

Photographic acknowledgments

The publishers wish to acknowledge, with thanks, the following photographic sources:

Environmental Images / Trevor Perry 26; Robert Harding Picture Library / M.H.Black - cover inset br; The Hutchison Library / Isabella Tree 7; Impact Photos / Dominic Sansoni - title page; / Piers Cavendish 12; / Maxine Hicks 21; / Neil Morrison 23, 25; / Brian Harris 27; NHPA / John Shaw 19; / Melvin Grey 28; / G.I.Bernard 29; Still Pictures / M Harvey - cover inset bl; / E.Robert/S.Bergerot 4; / Brecelj & Hodalic 9; / Mark Edwards 10; / Alain Pons 11; / Jorgen Schytte 13; / Roland Seitre 15; / Klein/Hubert 16; / Julio Etchart 17; Yves Lefevre / 20; TRIP / D Saunders 18; Woodfall Wild Images / Ted Mead - cover background, 22; Zefa 8, 24.

The publishers have made every effort to trace the copyright holders, but if they have inadvertently overlooked any, they will be pleased to make the necessary arrangement at the first opportunity.

Contents

What are wetlands?

Wetlands are places where the ground is wet and soggy most of the time. Some wetlands are often flooded with water. They may be near rivers or the sea.

The Okavango wetlands are in Botswana, southern Africa. This is one of the largest freshwater wetlands in the world.

Different types of wetland have different names. They may be called marshes, swamps, bogs, peatlands or muskeg.

These pictures show some different types of wetland.

peatland and saltwater marsh

floodplain wetland

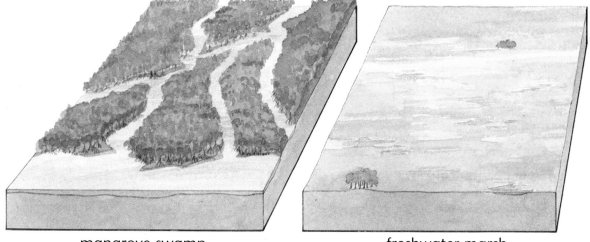

mangrove swamp

freshwater marsh

Where are the world's wetlands?

There are wetlands in most countries of the world. They may be in high or low places, and in hot or cold places.

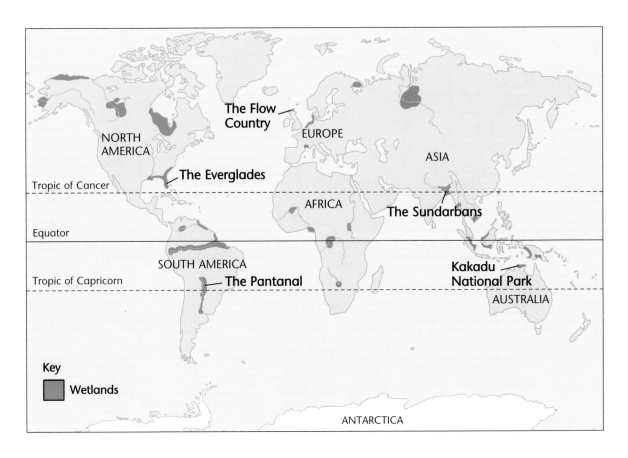

This map shows you where to find some of the largest wetlands in the world. You can see all the wetlands that you will read about in this book.

Different wetland **habitats** have their own plants and animals. They are all **adapted** to living in wet places.

Waterbirds live in all wetlands. Some of the world's largest **mammals** live in wetlands, too. The rhinoceros is a large wetland mammal.

These animals are a kind of water antelope, called a lechwe. They feed on grass, and live in wetlands in hot countries such as Botswana in Africa.

Using wetlands

Grasses, rushes and reeds grow in wetlands. These plants are used to make all kinds of things, such as baskets, boats and houses.

These are papyrus plants. They grow in wetlands in Africa. The ancient Egyptians used papyrus to make paper, as well as mats and sandals. People still use papyrus today.

In some wetlands people go fishing, boating and hunting. These activities may disturb or destroy the wetland habitat.

People have drained many wetlands to make dry land for farming or for building towns and roads. This has destroyed the wetlands.

Some wetlands are now **protected** from dangers like these.

This tin mine is in a wetland in Thailand. Waste from mines can poison, or **pollute**, the wetlands and kill wildlife.

The Sundarbans in India and Bangladesh

There are hundreds of small channels, or creeks, in the Sundarbans wetland. The people who live there travel mostly by boat along these creeks.

The Sundarbans wetland is partly in India, and partly in Bangladesh. It is a forest wetland area, where three big rivers enter the Bay of Bengal.

The mangrove forest here is the biggest in the world. Large mammals, such as the leopard, once lived in the forests. They have died out here because people hunted them. The tigers should be safe, because part of the forest is a tiger **reserve**.

The Bengal tiger is one of the largest mammals living in the Sundarbans. It is a good swimmer and hunter.

People who live in the Sundarbans take many of the things they need from the mangrove forest and the rivers.

The rivers are full of different kinds of fish. People catch fish to eat and to sell. They also hunt wild animals and gather plants from the forest.

People have cut down large areas of the mangrove forest for wood and to make farmland for growing rice.

The forest shelters the land from very strong sea winds, called cyclones. If more trees are cut down, the cyclones will cause more damage.

Rice is an important food crop. It grows under water, which comes from the rivers. Here women are harvesting rice.

The Pantanal in Brazil

The Pantanal is the largest **freshwater** wetland in the world. It is in Brazil in South America. The River Paraguay runs through it.

The Pantanal is a patchwork of trees, lakes and grasslands. There are few roads here so people mostly travel by boat.

The Pantanal is the most important habitat for waterbirds in South America. Birds stop here on their journey south from the Arctic lands in the north.

Many other wild creatures live here, such as the caiman and the capybara. The caiman is a kind of **reptile**. People hunt it for its skin, which is sold to make belts, handbags and shoes.

The capybara is the largest **rodent** in the world. It lives on land and in water, and eats grass. Its webbed feet help it to swim.

The rivers in the Pantanal often flood the flat land around them. People keep cattle on the dry grasslands which are too high for the floodwater to reach.

Farmers want more land for cattle **ranches** like this one. They clear the trees and drain the wetlands. This destroys the wetland habitat. Wild creatures lose their homes.

The rivers and lakes in the Pantanal are full of fish. Many people who live there catch the fish to eat and to sell.

Gold is mined in parts of the Pantanal. People use a **mineral** called mercury in gold mining. Then they wash the mercury away. It **pollutes** the waters of the Pantanal. Many fish are poisoned and die.

The Pantanal is changing. People have built dams and **reservoirs** there. This picture shows an electricity power station on the River Parana.

The Everglades in the USA

The Everglades form a huge freshwater marsh in southern Florida in the United States of America (USA).

The Seminole people once lived in the Everglades. They called the marsh 'grassy waters'. This picture shows why this is a good name for the area.

In the rainy season, Lake Okeechobee overflows and floods the Everglades.

To the north of the marshes is the Big Cypress Swamp. Cypress trees grow here in the wet, swampy ground.

The cypress trees are adapted to living in the wet ground. They grow 'knees' which are roots that stick up above the water to reach the air.

The grass that grows in the marshes is mostly sawgrass. Its leaves have sharp edges, like the blade of a saw.

The shallow ponds in the marshes are called ''gator holes' because the alligators make them. They scrape out the ground with their tails.

An alligator in the the Everglades

The Everglades marshes are smaller now than they were when the Seminole people lived there. Half of the marshland was drained to make farmland and land for building towns.

A small part of the marsh is **preserved** in the Everglades **National Park**. People cannot drain this marsh, or build on it.

People from nearby cities such as Miami like to visit the Everglades. They go boating and fishing there. Tourists visit from other places too.

Kakadu National Park in Australia

Kakadu National Park is in a wetland near the north coast of Australia.

This is a freshwater pool, or **billabong**, in Kakadu National Park. The park is famous for its wildlife.

There are many different wetland habitats in Kakadu Park. Near the coast there are **salt flats** and swamps. There are also freshwater marshes, and pools or billabongs.

Different plants and animals live in each habitat. There are almost 50 kinds of mammal, about 1000 kinds of plant and 5000 kinds of insect in the park.

Nearly 300 kinds of bird can be seen in the park. The magpie geese in this picture fly in huge flocks.

Aboriginal people have lived in the Kakadu area for more than 25,000 years.

These Aboriginal children are gathering shellfish from this billabong in Kakadu.

Thousands of tourists visit Kakadu Park every year. Most tourists go there to see the wildlife, or to enjoy the beautiful beaches and scenery.

Tourism has changed the wild habitat of the Kakadu wetlands. There are now roads and campsites in the park. Some people go there to hunt wild animals.

Twin Falls is a popular place for visitors. The best time to see the falls is in the wet season, from October to May.

The Flow Country in Scotland

Cotton grass grows on peatlands. You can see the fluffy white heads of the cotton grass in this picture. They are like the heads that grow on cotton bushes.

There are many peatlands in the British Isles. One of the largest is the Flow Country. 'Flow' means 'marshy ground'.

The Flow Country is a flat, windy area. It rains here much of the time, and the weather is usually cool. The winters can be very cold.

Peat is dead plant material which has not rotted away. The peat is soggy when it is wet and hard when it is dry.

When peat is cut and left to dry, it makes a very good fuel. Some people burn peat on fires and in stoves at home.

The plants that grow in peat are adapted to living in ground which is often wet.

Small lakes, or lochs, are scattered around the peatlands.

Many different kinds of bird live on the fish and plants in the lochs. The black-throated diver, shown in this picture, is often seen there.

Mosses, rushes, heather and grass all grow in the peat. They provide food for the deer, rabbits, birds and many other wild creatures that live there.

The habitat in parts of the Flow Country changed when people began to plant trees in these areas.

Many people **protested** about the tree planting. Now parts of the Flow Country are protected. No trees can be planted there, so the peatland habitat is safe.

Purple heather grows between the rows of young trees planted on the peatlands.

Glossary

adapted: if a plant or an animal can find everything it needs to live in a place, we say that it has adapted to that place. The animals can find food and shelter, and the plants have enough food in the soil and enough water. Some animals have changed their shape or their colour over a long time, so that they can catch food or hide easily.

billabong: in Australia, the word billabong is used for a pool or waterhole.

floodplain: flat land beside a river. When the river flows over its banks, water spreads out over the floodplain.

freshwater: water that is not salty.

habitat: the natural home of a plant or animal. Examples of habitats are deserts, forests and grasslands.

mammals: the group of animals whose young feed on their mother's milk.

mineral: something which we find in rocks or in the ground, such as gold. Minerals are usually taken from the earth or rocks by mining.

National Parks: laws are passed to protect these lands and their wildlife from harm. These places usually have beautiful scenery and rare wildlife.

pollute: poison. Polluted water contains waste materials. The waste may be poisonous and dangerous to wildlife.

preserved: saved or kept for the future. Preserved areas are kept safe from changes which would spoil or destroy them.

protected: kept safe from changes that would damage the habitat.

ranches: large farms where farmers keep cattle, sheep or other animals.

reptile: one of a group of animals which includes snakes, lizards and alligators.

reserve: an area of land set aside for wildlife to live in.

reservoir: a lake which has been specially built or used to store water for people to use.

rodent: a kind of animal that has strong front teeth. Rats, mice, squirrels and beavers are rodents.

salt flats: flat land next to the sea which the salty seawater floods.

Index